The Butterfly

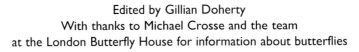

Edited by Gillian Doherty
With thanks to Michael Crosse and the team
at the London Butterfly House for information about butterflies

Illustrations copyright © Cathy Shimmen.
The right of Cathy Shimmen to be identified as the Illustrator of this Work has been
asserted by her in accordance with the Copyright Designs and Patents Act 1988.
First published in 2005 by Usborne Publishing Ltd, 83-85 Saffron Hill, London EC1N 8RT, England.
www.usborne.com Copyright © 2005 Usborne Publishing Ltd. The name Usborne and the devices ♀ ⊕ are Trade Marks
of Usborne Publishing Ltd. All rights reserved. No part of this publication may be reproduced, stored in a retrieval system,
or transmitted in any form or by any means, electronic, mechanical, photocopying, recording or otherwise,
without the prior permission of the publisher. First published in America in 2005. UE. Printed in Dubai.

The Butterfly

Anna Milbourne
Illustrated by Cathy Shimmen

Designed by Laura Parker

At the end of the garden,
there's a little stripy caterpillar.

What do you think
it's been doing all day?

First, it ate up the leaf
it was sitting on.

And when that
was gone...

it started munching
on the next one.

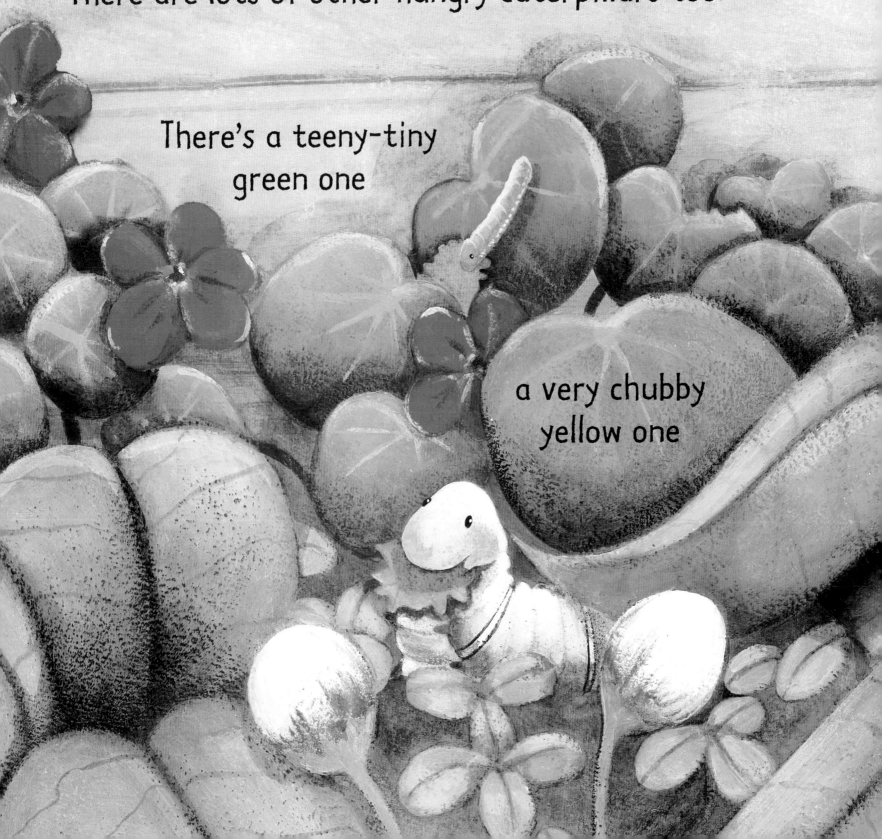

There are lots of other hungry caterpillars too.

There's a teeny-tiny green one

a very chubby yellow one

a soft, white hairy one

and a big, fat fuzzy one.

And all of them are eating as fast as they can chew.

The little stripy caterpillar is not so little now.

But **still** it keeps on eating...

munch

munch

munch

Soon it's even too fat for its skin.

So it shrugs it off, like it's just an old coat...

and then it eats
some more.

One day, the caterpillar stops eating.

Perhaps it's full.

It curls up under a leaf
and falls fast asleep.

Slowly, its skin becomes a shiny case.

It hangs there quietly, not moving at all...

for a very long time.

All at once it starts to wriggle.

It wriggles and wriggles
until the case splits open,
and it inches its way out.

The stripy caterpillar has become
a beautiful butterfly.

It stretches out its bright,
new wings in the warm sunshine.

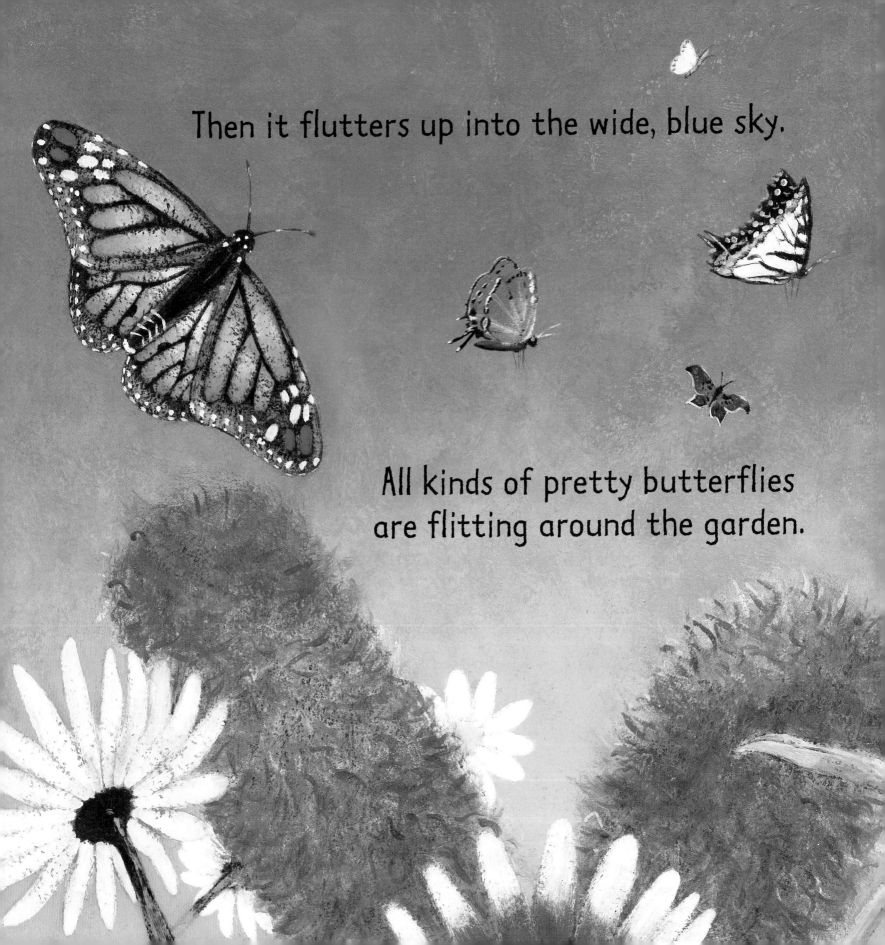

Then it flutters up into the wide, blue sky.

All kinds of pretty butterflies
are flitting around the garden.

There's a lacy white one

two speckled blue ones

and one with circles on its wings.

The butterfly flutters from flower to flower...

sipping sweet nectar
from every one.

At night, it folds its dainty wings...

and settles down to sleep.

When it's time, the butterfly carefully lays some eggs.

Each one is like a tiny pearl.

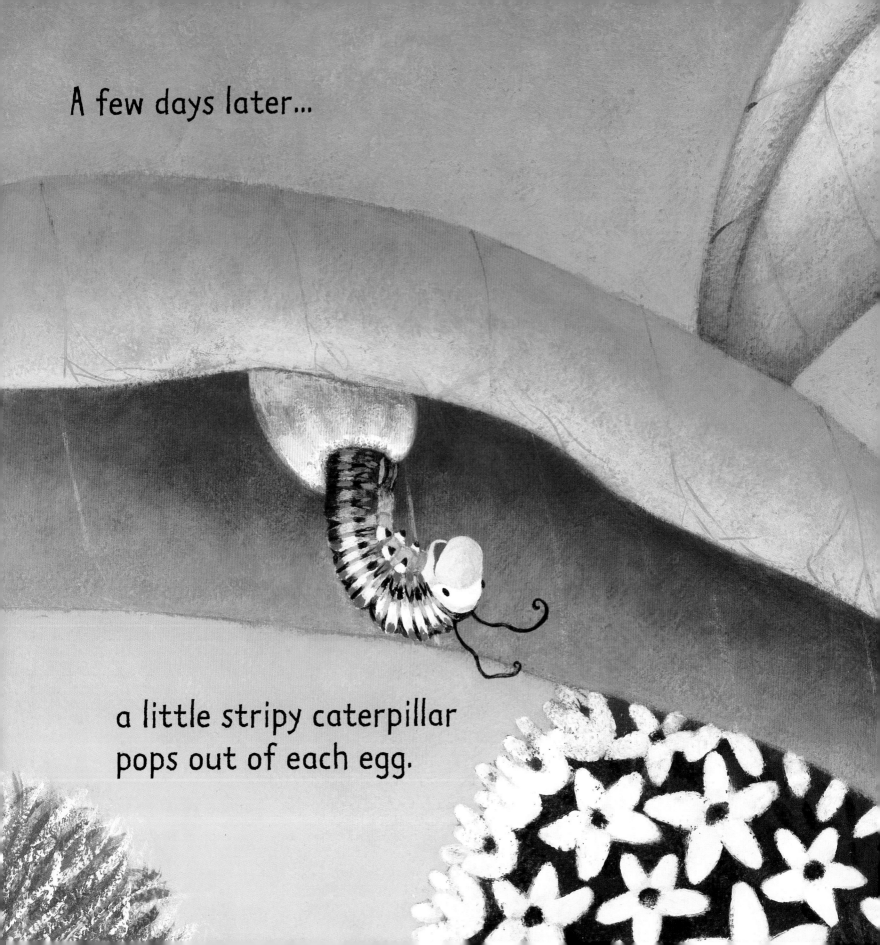

A few days later...

a little stripy caterpillar
pops out of each egg.

They are all
very, **very** hungry.

Can you guess what happens next?